HOURS AND HOURS TO COOK AND MINUTES TO EAT

ISN'T IT
ALWAYS
THE
WAY?

NATURALLY WE HAVE TO MAKE SOME SURPRISING CHANGES TO OUR ROUTINE WHEN THE CHILDREN COME TO STAY WITH US

This cartoon prompted a lot of observant readers to write and ask how it was that the car mirrors moved about from car to car. All very puzzling.

By a coincidence this cartoon appeared about the same time that Prince Charles bashed his finger driving in a stake in the garden. As one reader commented — Why didn't he get his wife to hold the stake like any normal husband would?

IT WAS SHAKESPEARE WHOTE — "IF ALL THE
YEAR WERE PLAYING HOLIDAYS, TO SPORT
WOULD BE AS TEDIOUS AS TO WORK"
NEVERTHELESS WE WOULDN'T MIND RISKING
A FEW MORE DAYS LYING IN THE SUN

ONE OF THE CHIEF REASONS THAT FLIVVER
AND MIGGY LIKE COMING TO STAY WITH US IS
THAT WE SPOIL THEM— LIKE LETTING THEM
STAY UP LATE TO WATCH TELEVISION

THE THING ABOUT
MODERN HAIR
FASHION THAT
PUZZLES GEORGE
IS THE WAY
GIRLS SPEND
SMALL FORTUNES
ON A SPECIAL
HAIR DO AND
COME OUT LOOKING
AS IF THEY'VE
BEEN PULLED
THROUGH A HEDGE
BACKWARDS

EVERY MARRIED COUPLE SEEM TO GO THROUGH A PERIOD OF THEIR LIVES WHEN THEY FEEL THAT THEY JUST CAN'T TAKE ANY MORE — BUT FORTUNATELY MOST OF US GET OVER IT

AND NOW FOR A FEW OF OUR LARGER CARTOONS
WHICH IF YOU LIVE IN BRITIAN IT IS VERY
UNLIKELY THAT YOU WILL HAVE SEEN BEFORE

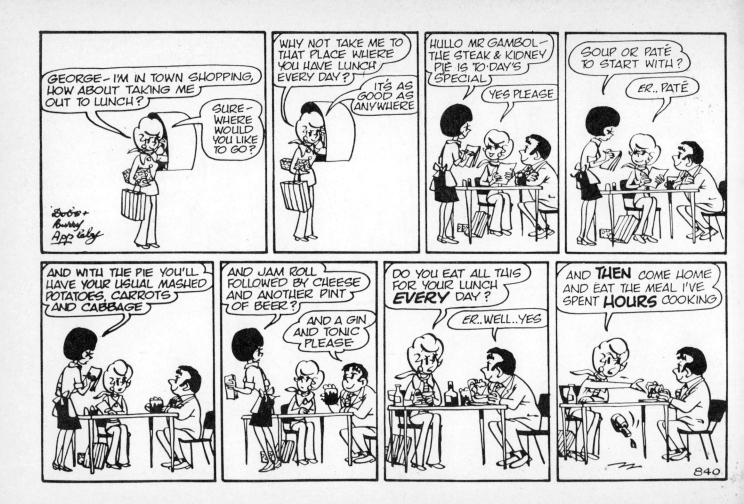

840

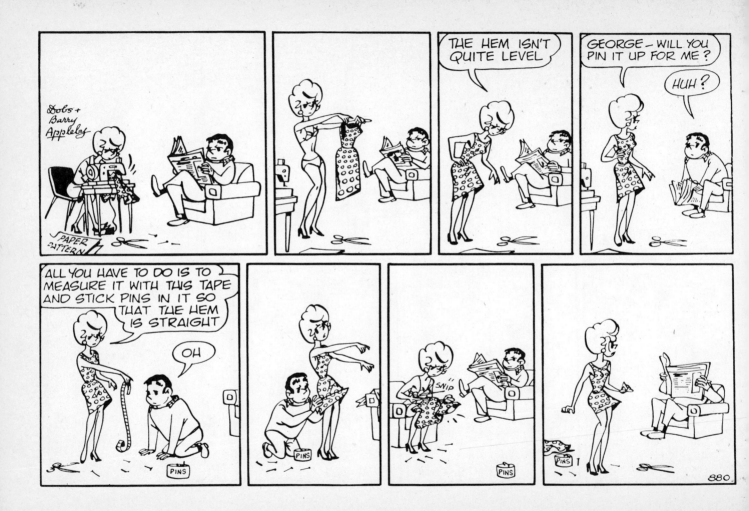

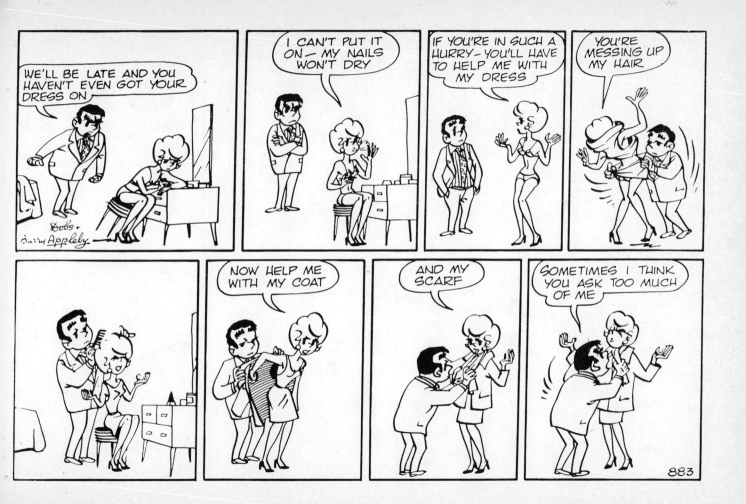

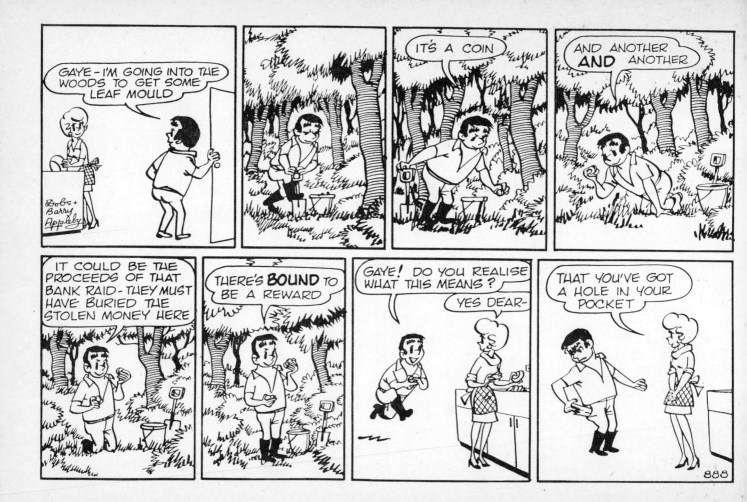

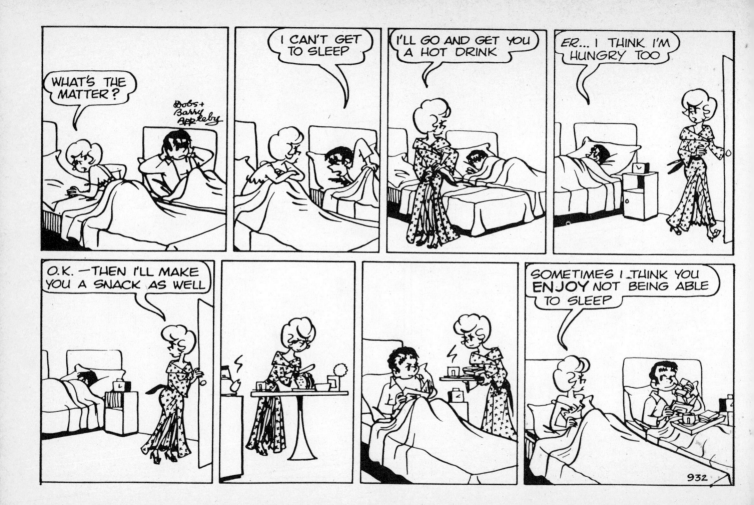

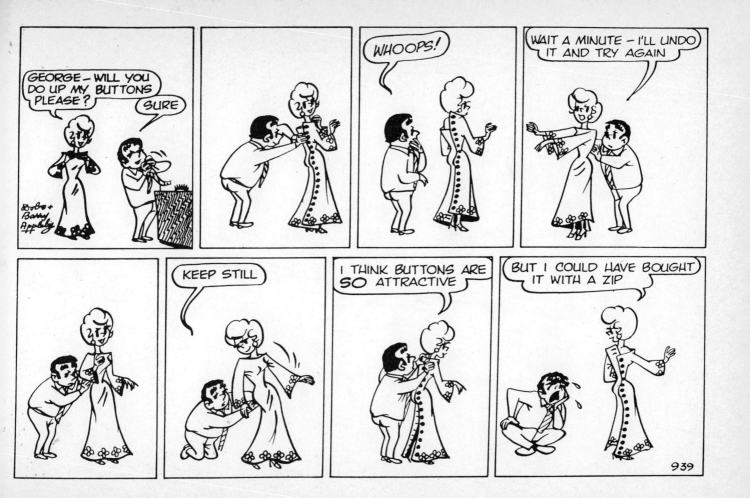

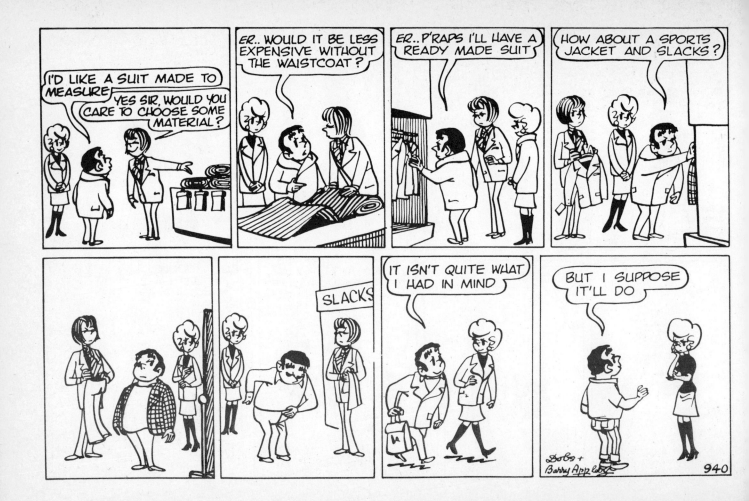

972

ONE THING ABOUT
GOSSIP IS THAT IT
DOES ADD A BIT OF
SPICE TO LIFE

YOU DON'T HAVE TO BE VERY OLD TO REMEMBER THE DAYS BEFORE ELECTRIC CALCULATORS WHEN ADDING UP WAS SIMPLE

IF YOU ARE FEELING DEPRESSED AND
NEED A PICK-ME-UP JUST PRESS THE
BUTTON AND STOP THE WORLD AT YOUR
COMMAND — WELL — IT'S ONLY A
SUGGESTION

THESE DAYS CHRISTMAS STARTS EARLIER, LASTS
LONGER — AND THERE ARE MANY MORE
PARTIES — ISN'T IT LOVELY ?

WELL — THAT'S THE END OF OUR
THIRTY-FIFTH ANNUAL — SO 'BYE FOR
NOW — SEE YOU IN THE MORNING

© 1986 *Barry Appleby*

Published by Express Newspapers Limited, Fleet Street, London, EC4P 4JT, and printed by Purnell Book Production Limited. Member of the BPCC Group